SIX
TRUTHS

Also by Sid Garza-Hillman

Approaching the Natural: A Health Manifesto

Raising Healthy Parents:
Small Steps, Less Stress, and a Thriving Family

SIX TRUTHS

LIVE BY THESE TRUTHS AND BE HAPPY. DON'T AND YOU WON'T.

SID GARZA-HILLMAN

Rare Bird
Los Angeles, Calif.

THIS IS A GENUINE RARE BIRD BOOK

Rare Bird Books
453 South Spring Street, Suite 302
Los Angeles, CA 90013
rarebirdbooks.com

FIRST TRADE PAPERBACK ORIGINAL EDITION

Printed in the United States

10 9 8 7 6 5 4 3 2 1

Library of Congress Cataloging-in-Publication Data

available on request

To Lisa, Luna, Rónán, and Rinah.

Contents.

INTRODUCTION

A note on pronouns.

Spoiler alert. As you'll read, I switch between he and she, him and her, and they. Randomly. No rhyme or reason, so don't go reading into it. Also, I'm switching between you, your, our, we, and so forth. We're all human and have way more in common than not. Let's not get mired in the minutiae, dig?

And now, we begin.

Everyone wants to be happy. Everyone. We certainly have opinions about choices a person might make to get there, but we absolutely want happiness, and as much of it as we can get.

So, with that understanding, let's go…

My story.

The trajectory of my life that led to my career as a nutritionist/health coach/running coach and this book is an odd and curvy one.

I graduated from UCLA with a BA in philosophy and a clear plan to pursue a career as a singer/songwriter. I took the first "day job" I could find, working at UCLA's audio-visual department with a bunch of other artists, writers, actors, and musicians who, like me, needed a semi-easy paycheck. Already by that time I had read several books on nutrition and healthy living after curing myself of asthma a few years prior by making a slight dietary change. As my music career progressed (much more on passion, struggle, and hard work later in this book), I found myself making a living as an actor and within about a year quit the AV job and continued working as a musician and actor for the next ten years.

Until…

Los Angeles began to wear on me and my wife, and we began to explore other places to live. Our first choice, Scotland, wasn't feasible, but my wife found the Mendocino coast and very soon we were on our way with a "we'll figure it out once we get there" mindset. In retrospect, not the most intelligent move, but then again…

Once settled in our new town and awake to the reality that we'd need to make a living, I got a job managing the restaurant at the Stanford Inn & Resort in Mendocino. The resort is anchored in sustainability and healthy living, and with my interest in nutrition I immediately felt at home. Over the next couple years I found myself in near constant conversations about diet, nutrition, and healthy living, but with no formal training, I felt I lacked "cred."

And so…

I made the decision to go back to school and become certified as a nutritionist. Joan and Jeff Stanford (owners of the resort) backed my decision and offered me the opportunity to teach classes, once certified (and, you know, insured). A year and a half later I finished the program and began teaching. Later I became the resort's wellness programs director, and still work in that capacity today. I have had two other books published, created an online habit change program (Small Steppers), direct an ultramarathon, and speak all around the US about my singular approach to and philosophy of health and happiness.

That about brings you up to speed. The bio at the end of this book fills in the particulars.

What I've found in the healthy/happy living arena.

As soon as I began working in the world of healthy/happy living, I stumbled upon a lot of nonsense. Over-complication, more information than most of us need to know, with a lot of fear tactics thrown in for good measure. I've taught many people over the years, given talks to many more, and have seen many a head on the verge of exploding from conflicting information, unsolicited advice, and an intense desire to have someone just tell it to them straight, in simple terms.

None of these people are stupid. The opposite, in fact. They're smart, but busy and don't want or need bullshit. They want truth and have a really good sense that happiness is simple in spite of the fact that they're being led to believe otherwise.

They are correct.

Everyone's endgame is a happy life. Happiness is the main highway, and we are just trying to stay on it as much as possible without getting detoured to side streets. Unfortunately, in the "how to be happy and healthy" arena, I see a reality time and time again: practitioners keeping people confused and/or afraid, and by doing so, they got 'em hooked.

Recipe for financial success as a health/happiness guru? Make it seem like you're trying to help your clients and followers stay on the happiness highway, but in reality, overload and overwhelm them so that they'll not only be stuck on side streets, they won't have a map. And just guess to whom those clients and followers will keep coming for directions. Yep. Every time.

Perhaps this explains why many a guru flies first class.

On the other hand, keep it simple and point people in the right direction—the direction of being able to create and maintain their own happiness—and they won't need you.

I much prefer this scenario.

Why I wrote the book.

I wrote this book because, from the depth of my soul, I believe the following two things:

1. If you're not happy and healthy, it may not be—and probably isn't—because you don't know enough. You probably don't need to read twenty more books or sit through ten more lectures. It just may be that it is about how you are or are not *using* what you already know.
2. Being happy is pretty darn simple. Hard and constant work to be sure, but not that complicated. Really.

A side note about health.

Because of my background as a health/nutrition/running coach, one might see this book as being about happiness AND health. But really, it is about happiness.

However, as I see it, health is a big ol' part of the happiness picture. As I've maintained from the beginning, a healthy body *and* mind are integral and essential to happiness. In fact, I'll arrogantly quote myself from my first book: "Caring for the mind is as important and crucial as caring for the body. In fact, one cannot be healthy without the other."

So…

You will notice health sneak in here and there on these pages. Best not to think about it too much, and instead just remember this: happiness above all.

The thing is, we simply don't need another flashy diet book or slick exercise DVD. Physical health is well played-out in the world (search for six-pack abs and/or keto diet on YouTube and you'll see). Instead, what's missing is a clear roadmap of how to be happy, how to live a happy life. Eating healthy food, while kickass, is only one part of that picture. Of course, diet books will keep coming because they sell better than philosophy books. However, that only makes them lucrative, not necessary or effective. I very quickly realized that every single client I had who came to me to talk about healthy eating really just wanted to be happier but was distracted by the shiny promise of a scale weight or six-pack abs. Truth is, those physical improvements and a healthy body? Mere *side effects* of happiness.

Get yourself *mentally* strong and happy, and a healthy body will come along for the very fun ride. Get yourself mentally strong and happy, and it'll be because you learned how to fundamentally treat yourself well, which will include how you feed your body.

Pretty simple stuff.

As it should be.

Because the *other* thing is, my main background is philosophy, and this, above all else, is what drives this book. Philosophy. More specifically, ethics and morality. Even more specifically, the right and wrong of how we treat ourselves. Treat yourself ethically and you are on your way to discovering what a successful life looks like.

The real challenges:

1. How to get there.
2. How to stay there once you get there.

Ultimately, being happy is a practice of self-care. Serious self-care. Hard-work-to-maintain self-care. The self-care that is built into the Six Truths that populate these pages.

It's about making yourself happy.

It's about you doing that.

For you first. Then for everyone else.

Incorporate the Truths and you will understand, possibly for the first time, the ramifications of caring about yourself on a very deep level. A thinking person's level.

Then, when you self-care for real, you will throw some positive influence into the world.

But that's later.

Now's about the learning and the work.

Now's got to be about you.

I distilled my years of working with and teaching people into these Six Truths. Of the many things I've learned, the one thing for sure is that we all desire a good life. We want to *feel* good.

This IS our core desire. People try to achieve it in a myriad of ways, but the big goal remains the same.

As different as we think we all are, it seems to me that the basic stuff—friends, family—is a very profound through-line. Technology and entertainment distract us, but happiness really is about a strong foundation of the basics.

Read the book, and then...

Read this book, get clear on your goals (the real goals), and only then and definitely not until then, get into the details. Fight like hell the urge to go down the rabbit hole of more and more information until, well, you're ready for it.

Of course, learning is great. It's just that it's a much smaller part of being happy than you might think. You lose if you're hanging out in the "I still need to learn more before I can get going" mindset. Nine times out of ten you know enough to at least get going.

In fact, you probably could've gotten going a long time ago.

But don't sweat that now 'cause time's a-wastin'.

Think about it this way... Digest the Truths, then consume the smaller details of food, exercise, meditation, journaling, guitar—hell, even sitar. Anything and everything that turns you on. These Truths will keep the big picture front and center as you're doing the smaller stuff. These Truths deliver the context. The perspective. The umbrella goals—the big goals that sit on top of smaller goals—that'll keep you from getting hung up on the details that distract most people. Anyone obsessed with hitting a number on a bathroom scale?

Hyper focus on the small stuff and you lose.

Here's what I mean…

If you think happiness is hitting a number on a scale or a skinny bod, you'll be grifted by whatever program promises to get you there the fastest. Follow that program and by gum you WILL get there quickly, if "there" is the scale weight. Problem is, without context, without an umbrella goal, you'll gain the weight back—with almost 100 percent certainty.

That is precisely the kind of thing that happens when you live without the big picture in your pocket.

Conversely…if you want to be happier, more vibrant, stronger, you'll avoid any bullshit quick fix programs like the plague. Quick fixes are for kids.

I call it "The Veruca Salt Phenomenon."

"I want it now!"

Really, Veruca? How'd that work out for you? And all for an *obviously* fake golden egg.

Instead, because you're an adult, you'll begin an adultlike

plan of improving the way you conduct the business of your life—how you eat, move your body, manage your stress for real. You'll take the necessary time to make new habits (trust me, usually takes longer than twenty-one or thirty days). You'll act from the truths in this book and then learn only what you *need* to know about what will get you to a happier, healthier existence. To hell with additional information or details beyond that.

Simply stated, with the big picture in your head, you will kick some ass instead of distracting yourself with information that is irrelevant to what you need to know to kick some ass.

Live by the Six Truths and you'll end up eating better, exercising smarter, working more efficiently, and social-izing for real.

You'll be running the show. Your show.

Directing your movie (figuratively or literally).

Controlling your life.

What's been missing and now isn't.

I wrote *Six Truths* to infuse into the world what is sorely missing from most conversations about living the best lives we can: philosophy and ethics.

I just hope, upon hearing "philosophy majors" announced over the PA at my college graduation ceremony, that I didn't stand up with my fellow, very small group of under-slept, over-caffeinated, slightly sweaty, old-Nike-and-torn-jean-wearing ragtag misfits for nothing.

The pages ahead.

What the pages ahead DO contain: philosophy, ideas, values, opinions, tools, definitions, perspectives.

What the pages ahead DON'T contain: fluff, case studies, charts, graphs, page-fillers, bullshit.

And, what the pages ahead ALMOST DON'T contain: anecdotes.

(I write "almost" because coming soon is an absolutely *classic* anecdote about the time I got fired from Domino's Pizza.)

One last thing for anyone afraid of being selfish.

To even endeavor to take care of yourself, to be selfish, to not put your own happiness on the back burner—the real, un-greedy, un-shallow happiness that this book is about—is noble, honest, authentic, and, most of all, necessary IF you want a better world than the one you're living in.

And since the world, and we humans, will *never* be perfect and can *always* stand to improve, the above statement is true whether it's 2020, 2120, or 2220.

And so…

With that…

Read on.

TRUTH ONE

Setting the example is *almost*
the whole shebang.

✳

Truth One is Truth One for a reason. The other truths have to come from this one. When you consider the other truths, incorporate them, make them your own, you can then let them go because they'll become part of this truth. This is the Truth you'll focus on.

Truth One will eventually become Truth ONE.

I'm being intentionally cryptic. Hang in there.

The truth(s) will be revealed by the end of this book.

The reason this truth eventually gets all caps is because ultimately focusing on it delivers a good life. The happy life. The life of depth. The life lived on your terms.

And you'll find out that following this Truth makes it so you don't have to talk about yourself.

Just an added bonus is all.

Al and Gandhi sitting in a tree.

I often quote Albert Schweitzer, who wrote that "example is not the main thing in influencing others, it's the only thing." I think Albert (I call him Albert) got really close, but not totally correct. Setting the example isn't the ONLY thing, but it is damn close and sure as hell the most effective thing. Gandhi's version, "be the change you want to see in the world," is right in my wheelhouse too.

While Albert's and Gandhi's words ring true, they have unfortunately, and in large part, remained mere words in today's world (kind of like how the whole "do unto others as you would have them do unto you" thing has been pretty much swept under the rug).

Not only is everyone so excellent at telling everyone *else* how they should be living, now there's social media and the "I'm automatically an authority because I signed up for a free Twitter account." Most of us are throwing words into the world with reckless abandon, with little consequence, and with little reason or incentive to actually practice what we preach.

Except...

Except that actually practicing what we preach delivers what solely preaching cannot.

Pedal the damn bike.

Most of us conceptually understand Truth One, but because we hate being wrong or admitting when we're not setting the best example, we deflect at every opportunity. We turn attention away from ourselves. We make *our* problems everyone else's. In doing so, we kick the "doing the hard work necessary to be a good example" can right on down the road (more on this in Truth Four). We just keep doing what we're doing without setting out to find a fix.

In a sense, we pull our feet off the pedals and coast.

But to be happy, we can't coast. We can never stop trying to be the best example we can. We can never stop trying to get better at practicing what we preach.

We can't coast. Not with ourselves, not with our relationships, not with our work.

We gotta always pedal.

I think the world could use a good kick in the pants about this.

Shut up until you can put up.

Me being blunt: People who aren't even attempting to live their words should shut the fuck up until they are living their words.

These people might trick us for a while (and some are masters at it), but the truth eventually comes out (usually).

And incidentally, the tricksters who spend all that time tricking are distracting themselves from the work it takes to actually live their words, which is SO much better than being a trickster (oh, just wait until Truth Four).

So…until they get that going they need to shut it.

And…

Once they get that going?

We might want to hear what they have to say.

Side note on perfection.

Perfectionists are boring.

Perfectionists have a hard time being happy.

A so-called "perfect" life, a happy life, is going to be full of imperfections, because humans are imperfect, which may be the understatement of the century.

However, just because we're imperfect by design doesn't mean we shouldn't at least strive for perfection.

As in, I think we can embrace our imperfection while shooting for the moon.

We'd all be much happier if we'd all continually approach perfection, even knowing that we'll never get there. Like, ever.

Voltaire said it best: *Le mieux est l'ennemi du bien.*

Translated from French to English is either:

"The perfect is the enemy of the good."

OR

"Your baguette is way better than my French toast."

(For this Truth, let's go with the first translation.)

Then again, who *really* knows what the hell perfection is anyway?

It just makes for a happy life to try for whatever you think perfect is.

The Subtle Cult Phenomenon.

If we gave our best effort to set an example of strength, positivity, health, and kickass-ness, we wouldn't get caught up in some other person's "way." We'd check ourselves long before playing the "pick a guru, any guru" game.

Why? Well, for one thing, "always follows a guru" doesn't set a good example.

Boom. Nailed it.

But our species has a problem, and it's what I call "The Subtle Cult Phenomenon."

The problem is how quickly we are able to put on blinders, believe without facts, and follow people over ideas.

I'm all in for learning from someone, but not for following someone.

There's a difference.

Following others gets kinda crazy and can very soon devolve into a cultlike relationship—one that may not be particularly obvious.

As in, it may be subtle.

Subtle because it not obvious like "robes" culty or "a compound in Idaho" culty.

But make no mistake, the subtle cult phenomenon *is* culty.

Fact is, when we follow someone else we hand over strength and power.

So…to illustrate.

Let's say you find someone who is living the example of what and who you want to be. Of course you are going to want to listen to what she has to say. Of course you're going to want what he's offering. You perceive that this person has figured "it" out, and that picture looks pretty darn good.

Fine.

But then let's say one or both of the following things happen:

You discover he's actually *not* living the example. For example, you find out the marriage counselor has been thrice divorced. The new age, meditating hippy has an anger problem. The spiritual guru sports a pretty hard-core food and/or drug addiction, or the staunchly pro-life senator just paid for his mistress's abortion. You know, just hypothetically...

Or

You reach a point where you have learned all you can (or at least enough) from this person.

Question is, what then?

What do you do *if* you want to live a happy life?

Ideally?

You move on.

To be happy, we all have to have the wherewithal, the strength, the character to take what we learn and do our best to...wait for it...live it ourselves.

The alternative is that we throw a "so what?" to one and two and just keep following the person.

Know what that is? A subtle cult.

And we just joined it.

When it stops being "here's what I'm doing" and becomes "I do what [insert name] does" or "I follow [insert name]'s program" or "I've been going to [insert name]'s retreats four times per year for the last ten years," you're probably in a subtle cult.

When you say, "Here's what I'm doing," even if what you're doing you learned from another person, you're on the right track. The track to happiness.

Being happy means ultimately erasing the teacher so you can take what you learned personally.

Listen and learn from people. Take what you need, chuck what you don't, make what you take your own, then take the person who said the shit in the first place out of the picture. I don't care how long his beard is or what magical powers he claims to have.

In case you're wondering, that goes for Buddha too. Thanks for some good ideas, Buddha, now I'm going to work on living them. *Unlike* so many of your "followers," by the way. Take care.

And yes, that goes for you too, Jesus.

John 13:15 "For I have given you an example, that ye should do as I have done to you."

Dang, Jesus just laid down some serious Truth ONE knowledge. If only more of his followers *lived* his ideas and values.

Yeah, I said it.

And I meant it.

One last piece of Truth One advice.

When you figure out what you stand for (see Truth Five), when you've incorporated ideas and made them your own, don't talk about stuff until you're either doing it or at least giving it the ol' college try. As tempting as it is, shut up about who you are and what you hypothetically can do until you're living it and doing it. Trust me, it'll be one of the best decisions you've ever made. The decision will force you to focus on YOU. All your ducks that have been uncontrollably flying around will finally be in a row. You'll be all about the real business of walking the walk. It'll be the self-kick in the ass that'll get and keep your life on the right track.

All the stuff you're not doing but wish you were doing? Figure THAT shit out before you try and convince someone else to do it first.

Here's a multitasking task: listen to those who are living a good example while working your ass off to be a good example.

At the same time.

One last piece of Truth One excellence.

Always trying to set the best example delivers you happiness regardless of whether you actually influence anyone else. It doesn't matter. It's not about that. It's just a great way to live and will save you hours of wasted time on social media sending wasted words into the world.

You'll be too busy getting better at being you.

But at the same time, the better example you are, the better the chances you'll rub off on others. Creating positive change in the world and all that jazz.

You'll positively influence family, friends, and coworkers way more by who you are than by anything you say.

Why?

Because setting the example is *almost* the whole shebang.

<u>TRUTH TWO</u>

Having a thick skin rules.
BUT...not too thick.

Spoiler alert. No snowflakes allowed.

I'm kidding. Snowflakes are welcome and if you're a snowflake, you need to read this. Your skin will thank you.

If you're not familiar with the term "snowflake," it means someone who believes they are super-duper special, and so fragile that they need to always be UNoffended, and at all costs.

At least that's my definition, and for the record, I've had to do my own hard, de-snowflaking (a word) work and still am.

Not to say we're not all unique. Of course we are.

In fact, live by the Six Truths and your uniqueness will come out in the best way possible.

And a bonus to boot: Whoever lives by these Truths won't expect anyone else to cradle him or treat her with kid gloves.

Fragility goes bye-bye.

Now that's one ass-kicking snowflake.

New age realities.

Here's just a smattering of new-age realities:

Trophies for every child, win or lose; no keeping score at soccer games with kids under eight; and helicopter parents—parents who hover, ensuring that nothing negative or hurtful ever gets in the vicinity of their children.

Result of these new-age realities? Thinner and thinner skins. Children growing up less prepared for the world, not more. Less equipped to deal with the inevitable pain-in-the-ass coworker, criticism, negative YouTube comment, or, God forbid, an opinion that doesn't line up perfectly with theirs.

Truth Two sub-truth.

You can't stop the negative. You can't stop bad things from happening.

Think about this: The thinner the skin, the easier it is for the negative to get through.

Logically, while thickening your skin won't prevent the negative, it will minimize the effect of negativity on your happiness.

Life actually is hard and there is a ton of unfair shit in the world.

It's simple. In order to be happy, we have to figure out how to be happy *in spite of* all the bad shit.

While it's that simple, it is supremely difficult.

The bad stuff is ubiquitous. The bad stuff populates the news. The bad stuff is clickbait.

We have to get and be strong enough to not let the bad stuff take us down.

A word on strength.

What is strength, really?

It's supremely important to define strength and know it when we see it because "strength imposters" are among us. Perhaps you've seen them: Men and women who wear a (very) public face of strength but who don't actually have it. They don't have it and no "faking it till you make it" will change that.

We need to define what true strength really is because if we don't know it, we could be imposters ourselves.

First, what strength ISN'T.

Strength ain't anger.

In fact, Truth Two was originally entitled "Strength is not the same as anger."

Seventy-four percent of the reason for that was that it's a lyric from my favorite English Beat song ("End of the Party"), and like most things English Beat has ever said, it is so, so true.

Anger and yelling only *seem* strong. But strength is not the same as anger.

Anger can even be the opposite of strength.

Anyone who yells all the time probably isn't strong enough. It means they've got some serious work to do in the strength arena.

Yellers often come on strong as a way to compensate for a profound insecurity and/or lack of confidence. Loud noises protect yellers from hard truths. Loud noises trick them into thinking they're strong.

Loud noises keep the truth nice and quiet, because sometimes, truth is a pain in the ass to deal with.

Makes sense, no? What's the best way to keep the spot-light off of you while simultaneously keeping the essential, painful truths about you hidden?

Go on the attack.

Make some big ol' tough-sounding noises.

If you're a dude, you might try sticking out your chest a bit. I've heard it helps.

But whatever you do, don't you dare budge or yield. Don't learn or grow. Don't change.

Don't listen, don't think, don't act. Only react.

Don't keep your cool, lose your cool.

I mean, if you listen, apologize, admit you fucked up, keep calm and cool, and maybe even change your mind, that's weak, right?

What strength IS.

Strength is cool, knowing, confident, principled, wise, listening, learning, caring.

Standing up when necessary and sitting down when necessary.

Strength is admitting when you're wrong and trying like hell to not be wrong again.

Strength is recognizing that while the insane "making zero mistakes" idea of perfection is impossible and therefore unachievable, you try like hell to achieve it anyway.

Strength is having a sense of humor and not getting bent out of shape at the slightest little comment, innuendo, criticism, or differing opinion.

Strength is the cool head in a sea of panic.

A skin only Goldilocks could love.

Strength and a thick skin go hand in hand.

But…beware…

There's thick and there's *too* thick.

Beware of a skin that is too thick.

True strength, and the happiness that comes with it, depends on skin that is just the right thickness. Not too thin, but also not too thick.

In today's world, too thick a skin and too thin a skin are both pretty ubiquitous.

And neither is good for the world.

In today's world, there is a serious shortage of just-the-right-thickness skin.

The Goldilocks thickness.

The Battle of the Skins.

Today's world is as divided as ever. Fractured, polarized, with everyone in their respective, extreme corners just waiting for the next round of fighting.

In the too-thick-a-skin corner? People with skin so thick they are incapable of change while simultaneously capable of some really bad shit. They are in constant protection mode. Buttoned up. Hiding behind a wall.

Reactive, and on the attack in order to deflect.

In the too-thin-a-skin corner? People who are offended. At everything. People who believe cancel culture is automatically ethical and moral. People who can't be friends or even friendly with someone who holds an opposing opinion. No walls, just all hanging out there, threadbare, waiting (hoping?) to be triggered.

Reactive, and on the attack in order to deflect.

Understand this: BOTH corners are anti-happiness and anti-strength.

And this: Achieve the right skin thickness and you're well on your way to happiness.

Oh, and this: Get there by building up or tearing down your skin as needed until it's just right.

If you're wondering how, fret not. You'll be reading some real-world advice very soon.

Here's where true strength comes in.

True strength is thinking for yourself regardless of if what you think is similar to or different from what others think.

It's both acting on principle and being open to change when you realize you've made a mistake.

Most importantly, true strength is not about what *looks* like strength. It exists on a deeper plane. Underneath and beyond appearances. It is so deep in the core of your soul that you don't need to even talk about it.

True strength is having nothing to prove.

It's speaking softly and carrying a big stick in a world that is increasingly about speaking loudly and carrying a small stick.

The truly strong fight to stop anger from ruling the day.

The truly strong definitely understand that compassion is a strength, not a weakness.

An aside.

Is social media not the perfect platform for the insecure, angry yeller? The troll? The tough-behind-the-computer-screen weakling? So, is social media at fault for the current state of affairs, or are *we* at fault for how much we use social media?

Yes.

Back to business.

Go just a thread's width deeper and it becomes crystal clear that when the angry-weak win the day, they don't "win" anything. Instead their actions breed even more anger and vitriol. In themselves. Their need to feel tough is never satisfied because they never actually become tough, thinking instead that being pissed will take care of it. A Twitter tirade, at best, provides a fleeting distraction from feelings of inadequacy. But make no mistake… Post-tirade, the feelings of inadequacy come right back because, well, the feelings were never gone in the first place.

The tirades and outbursts always wear off.

Their solution? Another tirade.

Our solution? Strengthen. And, for crying out loud, spend less time on Twitter.

Another side note.

Hey, News Outlets! STOP reporting on what somebody tweeted and instead actually report on stuff.

Do your damn job.

And Twitter, if you're reading this, please go away. You're annoying.

Trolls that give trolls a bad name.

The modern-day troll is the epitome of weak.

The strong, secure person doesn't troll. The strong, secure person doesn't even post a mean comment. In fact, the strong, secure person rarely comments, except to maybe throw down a supportive, nice comment on occasion. On occasion.

Why?

Because the strong, secure person has work to do. The strong, secure person creates, writes, expresses, acts. The strong, secure person's skin blocks the trolls. The strong, secure person exists on a higher level than the troll. The Troll lives under the virtual bridge.

A safe space for your emotional support pet.

The just-thick-enough-skinned person doesn't need safe spaces or emotional support pets. He doesn't try to censor differing opinions or stop people from talking. She either listens and considers or doesn't give a crap. This person calls the shots.

The strong person acts more than she reacts. He doesn't blow up at a situation, he handles it.

Fear and strength.

Being strong doesn't mean being unafraid. But it *does* mean being less afraid of being afraid.

The strong can feel afraid and succeed at the same time. Terrified of getting on stage, she walks on stage. Terrified of confronting someone, he respectively and non-reactively confronts someone.

Strong individuals know very well what happens when fear does the talkin', so they ignore it.

Know that every time fear calls the shots, a little more energy is sapped from your life. Less energy, less strength. Less strength, less happiness.

Now, back to the skin.

Having a thick, but not too thick, skin gives you a darn good chance of thriving in today's world, not just surviving in it. You won't need protection, you won't need to hide out, you won't let fear get the best of you.

At the same time, your skin is not so thick that you can't feel anymore. Not so thick that you can't empathize or see the other side. Not so thick that you become a shell of a human.

Successful humans feel stuff. The right stuff and the right amount of stuff.

The ol' kidskin.

When we can inhabit a "feeling fear but not beholden to it" state, we're primed and ready to raise our kids in a reasonable, non-freakish way. We are ready to raise kids to have the same kinda skin we have. No helicopter parenting, just parenting that produces strong, secure, compassionate children who will handle themselves in the world and be kind at the same time.

How do we hit the right skin?

So, the question remains: how to achieve just the right skin? How to get strong and stay strong?

Short answer first:

Come at it from all sides.

Long answer second, in three parts:

Part 1: Feed yourself well and move around. As in, take care of your body.

Part 2: Carve out time to think. Really think. By yourself and with no intentional noise around you. That means time YOU create by turning off music, podcasts, social media, friends, conversations, TV, news. Those things may be around you, but you're not the one turning them on.

As in input-free solitude. Silence isn't necessary, isolation isn't necessary. Just good ol' fashioned being in your own mind.

Here's where I blatantly steal from the book *Lead Yourself First*, which defines solitude as "freedom from inputs from other minds."

Such a great definition. Damn it, I wish I'd come up with it. If only I'd spent a little more time in solitude.

Once everything is turned off, except what's happening in your head, you get to *be* in your head.

Not to get hung up on semantics, but if you want to call this meditation, go for it. Meditation doesn't *have* to mean breathing, mantras, a little Buddha statue next to a candle, or being a "witness" to your thoughts. There is no meditation police that will bust you for not crossing your legs just so or placing your hands in some made-up-by-a-yogi position. That's all crap. I mean, go for it if that floats your boat—it's just not necessary. You can walk, run, swim, bicycle, or sit in a La-Z-Boy. But while you do…you process, think, consider. You build a practice of actively and intentionally thinking.

My good friend Jeff Stanford, a longtime meditator, calls this way of meditating "Thoughtful Meditation."

Such a great name. Damn it, I wish I'd come up with it. Again, probably could've used more solitude.

Here is a fact: If we are always stuffing information into our heads (hello, iPhone), we never actually *deal* with the information.

Here's a kickass analogy: Professional athletes do not train all the time. In fact, they're hyper-focused on recovery. Maybe even more focused on successful recovery than on the training itself. Recovery is when all the processing, rebuilding, and restoring occur. Recover well and the athlete can get out there even better the next time.

Here's another kickass analogy: intermittent fasting, which allows the body a substantial, daily break from eating in order to do its "business" more efficiently and effectively (repair, elimination, processing, building). If you're stuffing food in your body sixteen hours a day, when will it have the time and energy to actually deal with it?

Think of thoughtful meditation as recovery from very taxing information overload.

Part 3: Work hard and challenge yourself. Test your mettle from time to time. Push yourself more so you get pushed around less.

Stress? We need you.

What's coming may seem counterintuitive. Humor me.

Here goes: We need to stress ourselves out to become stronger.

But a special kind of stress.

It's called hormetic stress. It's the kind of stress that sparks your body and mind to strengthen. It's the goldilocks of stress. Just the right amount.

Side note.

What's up with me and Goldilocks? On some level I obviously believe she's underappreciated for her uncanny knack of nailing down when something is just right. Goldilocks: yet another unrecognized genius.

Humans have a very delicate relationship with stress. We don't do well with too little or too much, but we kick ass when it's in the right amount. Measured, intentional spurts of the extremes (too little or too much stress) can actually help us get stronger. But near constant, unintentional, extreme stress weakens us (see the cold/hot stuff below).

Too little stress and we stagnate. We get soft. We languish.

Too much stress and we burn out. We get soft. We languish.

Two sides of the same stressful coin.

But just enough stress—hormetic stress now and then—and our bodies and minds go into kickass mode. We don't languish. We rise to the occasion. We adapt, grow, learn.

I've done a good bit of research into and am a longtime practitioner of cold stress and heat stress—short stints of super cold (cold showers, ice baths) and super hot (sauna). Why? Because both are excellent examples of hormetic stress. By the way, exercise is too, and some breathing techniques will get you there as well. (For more on various hormetic stress strategies, see the resources section at the end of the book, but not until you're finished reading it all the way through. Seriously. Focus.)

The body undergoes amazing changes in response to hormetic stress—increased endurance and lean muscle, strengthened immune system, and even increased clarity of thought and a better mood. Trust me, all good stuff.

Hormetic stress is about thickening the skin. Toughening up.

Here's the crucial thing to understand. This is about conscious and intentional stress. Stress training, if you will. This is about intentionally inviting ourselves into temporary stress situations so that we are better equipped to deal with the stress that we *don't* invite, like family stress, financial stress, news stress, social media stress, pandemics, and more.

Again, being strong is never about avoiding the uninvited life stress, but about getting better at handling it.

Strength and compassion together at last.

The world needs more people who embody compassion AND a thick skin. Tougher kind people. That would be a happy frickin' world.

It's not that way so much now. Right now the assholes are dominating the skin game. The fringy/extreme populations are too damn loud.

Hopefully not for long.

A strong backbone.

The payoff of strength is huge. This Truth is a truth because real strength is the backbone of happiness. All the good intentions in the world mean squat if we're not strong enough to make them happen.

Meaning this: to be happy means being strong enough to be happy.

TRUTH THREE

Social media ain't social.

This Truth is a modern-era truth.

This Truth is a truth I can't believe I even have to include.

It's so obvious when you think about it even for a second.

Unfortunately, because we spend so much damn time on social media, we don't take the second.

The truth about tech.

This Truth is also a "technology won't save us" truth.

I know I'd be ridiculous if I thought all technology was bad. Of course it's not. It is a product of our incredibly creative, resourceful minds.

Here's what is bad:

Unchecked technology.

Technology divorced from philosophy. Technology without morality.

An example: Recently, I was told that a new restaurant was really "Instagrammable."

After I threw up a little in my mouth, I realized how nutty nut nut our culture had become.

What's wrong with "the restaurant's interior is super cool" or "the inside of the restaurant is really cute"?

Why does our experience of reality have to be filtered through a social media platform?

Tech in general.

Technology, from the remote control to the electric car window (thank goodness for that one by the way—our arms are a lot less tired), is aimed at making our lives easier, and that is certainly how most of us use it. If someone can invent something whereby we can achieve similar outcomes with less work, please get *that* done.

More tech, less work. Sounds good.

Except.

There are at least two very anti-happiness effects of more tech:

1. less thinking
2. less socializing

In this Truth, I take tech to the mat in hopes that you gain a little perspective on the ways it—and the ways we use it—is affecting us as a whole.

A refreshing look at heavy boxes and light boxes.

(There was a period of time during my junior year of college when I titled all of my philosophy papers with "A Refreshing Look at [whatever philosopher or philosophy]" for no other reason than to amuse myself. Not a single instructor or teacher's aide said a word about it.)

In my two previous books I framed healthy and nonhealthy behaviors using a gift-box metaphor. I won't belabor the metaphor here as I belabored the shit out of it in the other books. So instead here's a quick but sufficient synopsis…

Picture food as a gift box. A present.

In the food realm, the wrapping paper (or the box itself) is the calories (energy), while inside the box is the stuff that comes with the calories (vitamins, minerals, phytochemicals, antioxidants, fiber). So, the heavier/more substantial the box (i.e., the more of these nutrients that come *with* the calories), the healthier the food. A food's calories, like the wrapping paper on a present, isn't where it's at. The value of the food (and the gift) is all about what's inside the box.

Got it? And, as an aside, that's about as much as most people need to know about healthy eating, but instead they get mired in…wait for it…too much minutiae.

Mental food?

Well, the same gift box metaphor goes for what I call "mental nutrition," or what we feed our minds—all the stuff that goes into our heads like books, conversations, movies, podcasts, news, songs, and…social media.

Like food, not all mental nutrition is of equal quality. Some is healthy, some not, and a lot in between.

For example, while all novels contain words, they definitely are not all the same quality. As in, the fluff to the profound. The Steele to the Shakespeare.

Got it?

To be clear, I'm not anti-fluff nor anti–junk food. For me it's a matter of proportions—the proportion of fluff to profound or junk food to healthy food that we're shoving on in.

It's actually a very simple equation. To increase your own happiness, shove in more heavy box physical and mental food and less light box physical and mental food.

Now, let's get back to this Truth and the specific box I'm referring to.

For this truth, picture social media as the gift box. You know, instead of broccoli.

Why I quit all social media.

In December 2018 I quit all social media. Not just stopped using it, deleted it.

The main reason is that it didn't feel good. Plain and simple. It was soul draining, addictive, and a distraction from my work (including the writing of this book).

But also, I'd find myself seeing something beautiful while out running on a trail and my very first thought would be "would that make a good post?" I began to long for the days when I could just see something. Appreciate it in the moment. See the damn beautiful thing and maybe tell someone about it later.

So I quit.

Two things happened:

1. My career took a hit.
2. My happiness got a boost.

Fine.

I was okay trading number one for number two.

The work of socializing.

The overuse of social media is disrespectful to human nature. It's dishonest. In fact, the word "social" shouldn't even be part of "social media." It's a lie. It should be called "'a platform to see what your girlfriend from high school is doing' media."

With the word "social" in there, we *think* we're being social and connecting to other humans in a "human" way when we're tooling around Facebook or leaving a comment on Instagram. But we're not. Not really.

To be fair, there is something social-ish about social media, but it runs a very distant second to the real thing and is certainly not a substitute by any stretch.

The real danger of social media lies in its overuse. We don't tend to jump on for a few minutes then jump off. We don't take a moment to revel in the joy of communicating with a friend who lives thousands of miles away and then quickly return to our non-digital lives (incidentally, in researching this book I found out that you can also keep in touch with people by emailing them directly or even by eventually using the "sending a handwritten letter" technology that's currently in development).

Want to know why we don't just jump on and jump off social media? Because these platforms are specifically designed to prevent that from happening.

These platforms are designed to be addictive. We measure our worth by likes and they drip them to us in a way that we keeps us checking. And checking. We want the hormone hit we get from comments and likes, and in that desire, we ignore much of ourselves and the friends and family who are physically around us.

"Big rewards that come at unpredictable times trigger dopamine releases in the pleasure centers of our brains and keep us searching the web for the best price, trying to win an eBay auction, or pushing buttons on slots." (*The Atlantic*—see bibliography)

If you think social media is not addictive, quit Facebook right now. Should be fairly easy.

"Sid, I can quit any time I want."

Indeed. So quit.

Like right now.

No, really.

What it felt like to quit social media.

I did quit Facebook (and Twitter, LinkedIn, and Instagram), and twitched for about two weeks.

As I write this book, a leading cause of death in the US for kids ages ten to nineteen is suicide. One of the factors? Social media. Comparisons, partial representations, filtered pictures.

We may think we're more connected as a species, but in fact, we're more isolated.

We, and especially our kids, need to get out of the house more. If you're a parent, this is on you. I won't get into the essential parenting message here—for this, check out my book *Raising Healthy Parents* for a kind but substantial kick in the ass in the parenting arena.

Live by this Truth and you'll soon see how little social media has to do with socializing. You might not quit the whole enchilada, but you'll see the value in crafting a self-regulated, measured social media usage plan: a periodic check-in, but never a substitute for actual socializing.

And. You'll thank me.

The drug dealer in our pocket.

On-our-person technology is insane. As in the phone in our pockets or the tech watches on our wrists.

It is no longer solely about making the trip to a computer/laptop to search the net or jump on social media. Now, essentially, our computers are with us wherever we go. That means we can search the net and be on social media all the time. All. The. Time. That means we can also get the "hit" any time we want. It's like having a drug dealer in our pockets.

Just as having an actual drug dealer in our pocket wouldn't be ideal, having this little "tech drug dealer" isn't doing much good for us either.

The result of all this is that we take less and less time to think.

To clarify: It's not that we *have* less and less time to think. We *take* less and less time.

The difference between those two is significant.

So much information is being pushed into our heads, and so often, that we never stop and ask, "Wait, what just got pushed into my head?"

But…there's a cure.

It's first being aware of it so we can make physical, in-the-world moves to take breaks from our drug dealers.

"Hey, phone, stop trying to get me high all the time and park your ass on the counter a while."

The breaks deliver perspective. It's thinking. It's discussing. It's being around physical people.

One way to not compare yourself to someone's filtered/half-truth pic on Facebook? Have enough perspective to recognize how fake it really is. You can still check out the pic, you'll just be able to see it for what it really is.

But understand this about perspective:

You don't get it unless you stop and get it.

And once you do, one thing will become crystal clear:

Social media ain't social.

TRUTH FOUR

There is no substitute for hard work
and there never will be.

※

In the early days of my music career, I spent a decent amount of time wishing I'd get a big, old, appearing-on-my-doorstep break. Hoping success would come in some magical way, or that maybe I'd discover some hidden talent I didn't know I had, but when I found it, would set me up for life.

Financially at least. (Oh, just wait for Truth Five.)

I mean, I understood that I'd have to do *some* work, but with the magically delivered talent and/or break I figured it wouldn't be *hard* work.

Eventually, I did get a break.

The break was learning that hard work, and I mean hard work, is an integral part of success.

Actual success.

The kind that leads to happiness.

Not the viral YouTube video kind.

Side story.

I once interviewed a girl for a job who made sure to let me know she had a viral video on YouTube, which, I'm assuming, she believed was something I should seriously factor into my decision whether or not to hire her.

The video?

A dog trying to pull off her bikini.

Millions of views.

And, no surprise here, I thought, Why *wouldn't* I hire someone with millions of views from people who clicked on a video to see a dog try and pull off a girl's bikini?

While times they are a-changing, this Truth won't ever change: It takes hard work to achieve anything of value.

True success can never and will never be handed to you for free.

Turns out that even if you do have some hidden, awesome talent, you still have to work your ass off to be successful with it.

You can't remove hard work from success.

Hard work and success are inextricably bound and we'll be a lot happier when we just accept that this Truth is, well, true.

Take a long, hard look at a few realities.

First reality: by trying to avoid the stress of hard work, you'll cause yourself even more stress.

In other words, you'll miss out on some good times if you try to cut corners, search for hacks, or sit in your house waiting for happiness and success to magically appear. You'll never know what it feels like to earn what you want or the happiness that comes from even trying to get it.

Second reality: You can't really relax until you've *earned* relaxation.

What's that thing I just wrote about relaxation?

We're all about time off these days. Social media is time off. TV shows are time off.

It's fine to take time off, I'm just saying it's way more enjoyable if we bust our asses off before we take it.

After a hard day's work you will *know* what relaxation really is and here's why: because you won't be thinking about all the shit you didn't even try to get done because either you got it done or worked hard trying to. At that point, social media and TV can be for fun and not distractions from all the shit you didn't try and get done.

See the difference?

Kinda like with healthy eating.

I coach people how to eat heavy box food *most of the time* (I call it "the MOTT" because I like abbreviating stuff) for two reasons:

1. Eating healthier most of the time makes them healthier
2. They stop feeling guilt and shame if/when they eat a little junk food once in a while. Amazing how much better food is without the aftertaste of guilt and shame.

Fine, you asked for it. A smoking analogy.

I once asked a chain-smoking friend if he enjoyed cigarettes. "No," she replied.

Know why? She smoked so frequently she was no longer aware of the act itself. Smoking had become something she *had* to do, not something she enjoyed.

What Big Macs and smoking have in common.

Big Macs and smoking have this in common: they both alleviate stress in the short-term.

Big Macs and smoking *also* have this in common: they both do NOT alleviate stress in the long-term.

Big Macs and smoking also have this in common: I so love(d) them both.

Momentary stress reduction vs. long-term stress reduction.

Alleviating short-term stress with Big Macs and ciga-rettes is easy.

Really taking care of yourself is hard work.

That's precisely why it's better.

And now, back to the realities.

Third reality: Hard work keeps the fight in you

Ever read the bumper sticker "you can sleep when you die"?

Yeah, it's stupid given how crucial quality sleep is to stress and happiness, but…

There is a little nugget of truth hidden in it.

A quick aside.

There should be fewer bumper stickers. In general, in the world. There's just too damn many. They're like mobile social media comments and I'm sick of 'em.

Glad I got that off my chest.

Back to the third reality.

The nugget of truth is that hard work—and accepting the necessity of it to be happy—keeps you fighting. Keeps you engaged in living the best life you can for the entirety of your life. Keeps you…happy.

Better bumper sticker: You can stop working hard when you die.

Or something along those lines but please don't make it into an actual bumper sticker. Don't get me started.

Ageism.

One of the worst things to hear is "I'm too old to do that" or "that's just what happens when you get older!"

All ways of saying "I've lost the fight" and certainly not fair to the older folks who are still fighting (more on the so-called "elderly" in Truth Six).

So, keep working hard and never lose the fight.

Fourth reality: The happiest you are, or will be, will be as a result of something which you worked your ass off to get.

In any and all areas of your life. Work, family, art, friendship, self-care.

And, perhaps most importantly, the hard work of honesty, awareness, principle, integrity, communication.

Example: the hard work necessary to maintain a successful relationship.

Marriage without work is doomed to fail. Parenting without work is doomed to fail. Friendship without work is doomed to fail. A coworker relationship without work is doomed to fail.

Every kind of hard work pays off. And, yes, some hard work you get paid for. But the "non-money-getting" work kicks more ass because you get paid in happiness.

Get it?

The problem with hard work.

The problem: We *think* we don't like it and will do our darndest to avoid it.

Diets, exercise plans, and other "quick fixes" sell because they promise results without hard work. They sound in-credible! Literally, in-credible.

The more you incorporate Truth Four, the more you'll seek, and I mean actually seek, hard work. Anything or anyone promising easy happiness will be a giant red flag or in the very least a big ol' bottle of snake oil. Choose your metaphor.

People on the lookout for easy happiness aren't happy.

Talk to any yo-yo dieter, and they'll tell ya.

Lo and behold.

Understand Truth Four and lo and behold….

1. You stop worrying about hard work.
2. You stop causing yourself stress by trying to avoid hard work.
3. You are happier.

Why is this Truth true?

I'm interested in why this Truth is true. What is it about us that makes us happiest when we're working hard, engaged in body and mind?

Hold on, I'm not that interested.

Because.

This Truth is just true.

If you want to be happier than you are right now. Work harder.

If you're marriage isn't making you happy, work harder (yes, your spouse should work harder too, but revisit Truth One for crying out loud).

If your job is unfulfilling, work harder.

If you feel unfulfilled, unsatisfied, or unrecognized, get the hell off social media and get to work.

On a book, a song, a painting, a ceramic coffee mug.

Run, walk, swim, hike, bike.

Put your body and soul into something and see what gets kicked back out at you.

Actors who don't act.

A young woman once asked me for advice about acting and the acting business (I used to be a working actor) because she had dreams of moving to Los Angeles to act.

I gave her a few acting books that had helped me hone my craft along the way. I told her to check them out and see if any of the various methods/exercises piqued her interest.

But then, I said… (and I'm paraphrasing myself):

"Don't get too hung up on the books and don't get too hung up on acting classes. Read them, take them, sure, but the *first* thing you do as soon you step foot in LA? Start working."

Start working as an actor.

In other words, don't kick the "acting can" down the "acting road" because you think you have to wait until you've read five acting books, found the perfect acting class, or are graced with an audition for a Cheetos commercial.

Start acting immediately.

But, Sid, how can she be a working actor without being a working actor?

Here's how, and what a great question you probably didn't ask.

She can write a one-act play (even if it's not so good and she knows it), learn it, set up her phone on the table, hit record, act it out, watch it, and critique it.

Then do it again.

And again.

When she inevitably meets other actors (it's Los Angeles—she'll trip over them much like I trip over marijuana growers where I live), write more one-acts or grab scenes from the internet and act them with other actors, again, on the phone's camera. Watch them as a group, critique each other, then do it again.

And what a cool way to use your cell phone, no? In fact...

Technology for the win.

I know I don't paint a pretty picture of technology in Truth Three, but I did say it ain't all bad. In fact, there is some technology awesomeness, like…

The cameras on our cell phones, iMovie and Garage-Band on our laptops, not to mention writing and drawing apps, and way, way more. Accessible, cheap (in fact, mostly free), and relatively easy-to-learn tools that facilitate creativity—photography, acting, songwriting, novel writing—all in that little, mostly annoying, rarely-used-for-cool-stuff phone in our pockets.

Here's the hitch: They don't use themselves.

Pro-gram does not equal pro-fessional.

Understand this: Having a pro-gram on your computer doesn't make you a pro-fessional.

Having GarageBand doesn't make you a professional musician any more than Final Draft Pro makes you a screenwriter, Adobe InDesign a graphic designer, Premier a filmmaker, or a kickass iPhone camera a photographer.

Only one thing makes you a professional…the work itself.

If you're thinking, "No, Sid, getting paid makes you a professional!" you got another think coming.

Nowadays, most people have incredible tools. Very few produce.

Ab-cruncher, roller thingy, anyone?

This all sounds a lot like the used-twice, gathering-dust-in-the-garage infomercial exercise equipment that we thought would magically get us those six-pack abs, no?

Here's what you can do instead of ordering another stretchy, roll-y, shaky exercise thing: Walk out your door, then run a bit, then walk some more.

Repeat that a while and then, maybe later, buy some fancy shoes. Dig?

A tool sub-truth.

Tools don't use themselves.

This fact ain't gonna change, no matter how much you want what you want handed to you sweat-free.

But, again, this is actually good news.

Why?

One more time: You are happiest when you work for your happiness.

When you earn it.

Hard work is in our DNA.

Our bodies and minds love it.

Just because a lot of technology tricks us into thinking we don't love it and don't have to work our asses off to be happy doesn't mean we don't.

The Should Cloud.

What do all of the following people have in common?

Screenwriters who don't write screenplays, songwriters who don't write songs, novelists who don't write novels, photographers who don't take pictures, vloggers who don't vlog, podcasters who don't podcast, runners who don't run, healthy eaters who don't eat healthy, gym class–goers who don't go to the gym, entrepreneurs who don't start their businesses?

This:

They are all living under what I call "The Should Cloud."

People living under The Should Cloud say things like:

> "I *should* work on my screenplay."
> "I *should* work on my music."
> "I *should* write my novel."
> "I *should* vlog."
> "I *should* exercise."
> "I *should* eat better."
> "I *should* start my business."

And, I'll bet a bunch of money on this:

They're not happy living under The Should Cloud.

And this:

They would be happier if they were actually doing the things they think they "should" be doing.

Why? Because every single time they actually did stuff, they'd be stepping out from under the cloud.

Fake it till you make it? Holy crap, that's idiotic.

I know, I know…conventional wisdom says fake it until you make it. I have a problem with most conventional wisdom.

What this means is:

Act like a rock star until you actually become a rock star.

Walk around acting like a famous actor, and by gum, you'll eventually be a real-life famous actor.

What a crock of shit.

Allow me to clarify.

Maybe acting like a famous actor will get you attention or an extra-special audition.

Maybe acting like a rock star will eventually garner you the attention of millions.

If that's your bag, buy a book about how to act like a rock star and read it. This is not that book. This book is about becoming happy, staying happy, and kicking ass.

For the record, you can be a rock star AND be happy and kickass.

But not because you faked it till you made it.

Happiness comes from trying to make it and not wasting an ounce of energy trying to *look* like someone who already has.

Every moment spent faking it is time away from making it.

I nailed it with that last sentence. Admit it.

Don't be a Sideliner.

In this social media, Yelpy, "everyone can comment so therefore everyone should be heard" age, *everyone* knows how to do everything better than you can and spends a ton of time commenting on what everyone *else* should do. (It's like they're moving the Should Cloud off of themselves and on to everyone else. That's not frickin' fair.)

And yet...

These self-proclaimed authorities certainly talk a big game but more often than not don't get into the game itself.

I call them sideliners. People who yell from the sidelines of the game.

Sideliner.

Don't get me wrong. I get the draw of being a sideliner. I'll watch some sucky YouTube video and feel the urge to leave a comment about it.

And then I tell myself... "don't be a sideliner."

Why?

I'm only one guy. One guy, one opinion. One guy, one opinion, one perspective. Small change in the big scheme of things.

And, more importantly, the YouTuber didn't asked for my opinion.

And also, if I have time to comment on someone else's work, I have time to work harder on my own.

In other words, I need to shut my trap and get back to work.

If I don't like someone's work, I don't have to keep looking at it.

When we see someone else's work we don't like, we feel (in our totally misguided, overestimated sense of self-importance) a need to "fix" it. I guess in order to save the rest of the world from having to see anything that doesn't meet *our* standards…

Everyone's a critic, and all that jazz.

Why I turned my YouTube comments off.

Following my own advice (Truth One, anyone?), I disabled comments on my YouTube videos.

As much as I liked seeing the positive comments, it was the one-off nutty nut nut, negative comments that bothered me.

It's always the one negative in a sea of positives that tanks us.

So, I had a choice to make. Let 'em all in, or shut 'em out.

I chose the latter for the same reason I quit social media, and stopped reading comments on my podcast and books (yes, including this one).

Freedom of speech should always be valued and defended. But, so should freedom of listening. As in, just because you have the right to say something doesn't mean I have to listen do it.

Plain and simple, yes?

Try keeping comments to yourself, BUT at the same time, take note.

I offer you a silver lining on the whole urge-to-comment front.

Turns out watching the crappy video was *not* a waste of time. You just found out more information about what you like and don't like.

It's great to make judgements, to have opinions, to concretize what you like and don't like in the world. But use these judgements to improve your own work rather than leaving them as comments on someone else's.

Everyone has great ideas. So what.

Ideas are so commonplace. They've become boring.

Every so-called screenwriter in every Los Angeles coffeehouse has one.

Ideas are dime a dozen.

But there's something way more exciting and definitely worth more than a dime a dozen. Someone who makes something out of an idea.

Someone who takes an idea and makes it real. In-the-world real.

Takes an idea and…

Turns it into the screenplay, regardless of whether anyone ever reads it or likes it.

Turns it into a song, regardless of whether anyone ever hears it or likes it.

Turns it into a video, regardless of whether anyone ever sees it or likes it.

Turning an idea into a reality is fucking exciting.

So…two things:

1. Stop. Talking. About. Your. Amazing. Ideas.
2. Start. Working. On. Them.

Execute the idea.

I find it odd, and a little unsettling, that the word "execute" has these two meanings:

1. to carry out/put into effect
2. to put to death

However…I thought about this a good long while (in solitude, dig?) and came to this conclusion:

Executing an idea is doing this:

PUTTING AN IDEA TO DEATH AS AN IDEA.

As in, when you make something real out of an idea, it's no longer an idea, right?

One last thing on this Truth.

Remember how working hard keeps the fight in you?

Well, that's true NO MATTER HOW OLD YOU ARE.

Apply this Truth and you will never ever languish. You will never ever be bored. You will never ever stagnate.

Ever.

This Truth guarantees a pretty damn good future, wouldn't you say?

If you accept that hard work is a key variable in the happiness equation, you'll be happier.

Do the math.

TRUTH FIVE

The more aware you are of
what you give a crap about,
the happier you'll be.

✳

"No duh, Sid," you say?

Think this Truth is obvious?

Think again.

Turns out we care about stuff we don't really care about.

Of all six Truths, this one takes a bit of getting used to. It's tricky, sneaky, and the Truth we *think* we have a handle on but often don't.

Here's an example.

Ever get swept up in some office drama? Probably. We all have.

But...have you ever had the moment, perhaps back home that evening, when you think, "Why did I give a flying crap about that?" or "Why did I get all bent out of shape about it?"

Look, while you may love office drama, gossip, and *People* magazine, you may, you know, not *actually love* those things.

Maybe those things are distractions. Maybe they merely help pass the time.

But maybe, just maybe, you don't actually care about any of it. Not in any meaningful way.

At the very least, Truth Five is about giving everything you think you care about a second (or third) look. This Truth is about the profound value of finding out and defining, in a profoundly real way, what the hell you give a crap about.

Here's why…

What you *do* give a crap about.

Without a keen awareness of what you care about, you'll end up wasting precious time on stuff *and people* you don't care about.

An aside.

Wait…people?!?

Yes. People.

I'll bet there are people in your life right now that suck some of your precious time and energy away from you.

Including people in this Truth may be a little harsh. But you'll get no apologies from me as it's frickin' true.

Of course, no need to be mean to them or show them any disrespect (what kind of example would that set, right?). But it's good to know you'd be happier if you spent less time with them.

Once you know, you're better equipped to make moves as needed. Dig?

What you *don't* give a crap about.

Just as important as knowing what we do care about is knowing what we *don't* care about.

As in, good to define both the do and the don't. So we intimately know both.

The question is this: Is our happiness proportionate to how focused and aware we are of what does and does not matter to us?

Absolutely.

Holly's hobby.

Over the years, in various work settings, when I watch someone (or myself) get swept up in some ridiculous office BS or some other mundane drama, I have this intense urge to say "get a hobby."

As in, build more of a life *outside* the office so that you/I can see that what happens *at* the office really isn't all that important. As in, bring in more extracurricular, fulfilling work (or, literally a hobby) into your life until the unimportant stuff becomes even less important.

On that note, a little tidbit about me:

Let's just say there have been plenty of times I've needed to "get a hobby."

From time to time, when I find myself distracted by bullshit, I remind myself to focus even more on the (ton of) more important things in my life.

Do the math.

Try this:

Document the last five times you've been involved in a work-related drama.

Now, ask yourself this question about each of the five times—did I *really* care about it? Like, *really*?

There's a good chance you didn't care about at least four of the five.

This is some seriously good information to have if and when you make moves to improve your life. With this info you stand a better chance of not being reeled in by some stupid drama that is, frankly, beneath you.

It ain't worth your time.

So, what is worth your time?

Stuff you care about.

Blessed are the distractions.

Distractions are unparalleled in the world today.

It is just so damn easy to spend our non-work lives glued to a screen.

I call it the "extracurricular distractional reality" and it inflicts serious damage to our happiness.

For the record, I don't care that "distractional" isn't a word (because I know what I do and don't care about).

With too much of the extracurricular distractional reality, we can too easily look up from our screens a year from now with no novels written, no healthy eating under our belts, no miles under our feet.

Too much distraction turns us off from our lives.

For the record, I'm not anti-break.

As I've said a thousand times, we all need a break from time to time.

Problems arise when two things happen:

1. there is more break time than *work time*
2. there is more break time than *think time*

If you do the hard work of building quiet, non–distrac-tional time into your life that tips the scales in your favor, you, well…tip the damn scales in your favor.

In other words, if you can spend most of your time on what you care about because you took the time to find out what you care about, you win.

At that point, *happily* take breaks if and when you need them.

The people win.

Incidentally, when you spend more time on what you really care about, the people in your life win.

Follow along with my self-proclaimed, impeccable logic:

If you spend more time with the people you really care about because you're more focused, less distracted, and happier in general, the result is that they all get to be around a great version of you.

Boom.

Excitement is exciting.

Gaining all this awareness is easier said than done because those damn distractions are so tempting. They get us all excited. They light us up in the moment.

Let's face it, excitement is exciting.

But don't make this mistake:

Don't confuse excitement with happiness.

We get all *excited* about diets, DVD fitness plans, trips, parties, and more.

We all do.

Those things *are* exciting, for crying out loud.

But there isn't much happiness found inside that stuff.

Happiness lives in the day-to-day. In the baseline of our lives, not in the temporary spikes of excitement.

The spikes are fun, but they don't deliver day-to-day happiness.

On the other hand, improve the baseline, make your days full of awareness, work, and all the stuff you care about, and you'll be happy.

Then, just like taking well-earned breaks, go ahead and throw in some spikes: adventures, classes, diets, races, and DVD fitness plans.

But don't confuse excitement with happiness.

You *can* have both. Just don't confuse the two.

Have you got the solution?

I've got the solution.

I've got the solution of how to build in more thinking and awareness into your life.

Here goes:

Put down this book for fifteen seconds and stare at the wall.

That's the solution.

The solution is more silence.

Silence delivers the framework inside of which we can get our heads on straight.

Sounds (no pun intended) pretty simple, no? Just grabbing a little quiet?

Easier said than done, and it's not getting easier.

Silence is a rare commodity these days. We are surrounded by a shit ton of noise all the time.

Yes, the house, the car, the office, the coffee house, the subway, the bus, the bar, are all noisy, but…

If left unchecked, what crowds our brains more is the stuff we turn on ourselves like podcasts, videos, TV, music.

And then there's the non-noise noise.

Wait, non-noise noise?

Most social media is a perfect example of very loud non-noise. We hear all those petty, troll-y, nasty comments in our minds, don't we? Reading the news? Texting? Non-noise noise as well.

We are not victims.

We *can* grab silence.

Just because we don't doesn't mean we can't.

We don't have to *always* have the podcast, the music, the TV, the social media, and the texting active all the time.

Delay the inevitable.

Here's a very useful "grab some silence" tool.

Kick the "noise can" down the road by waiting just a bit before hitting the proverbial "on" button.

(I've always loved that "on-button" proverb.)

Here's what I mean:

Just for a few minutes, while in line waiting for your latte, don't look at a device, talk to a stranger, or read the newspaper. In doing so you buy yourself a little respite from the stuff that everyone so often pushes directly into our heads.

Bonus: The little respite is much cheaper and more valuable than the $4.71 latte you just stood in line for.

Even delaying noise is a great way to steal some thinking time without feeling like you're giving up anything. In other words, delaying for just a few minutes isn't about not looking at the screen at all. It's about waiting a little longer before you do.

In this way, there is no need to pull the old standby: "You're not the boss of me."

I'm not taking away your toys, I promise.

Silent *enough*.

If nobody is talking to you, you're not staring at a TV or computer screen, and you don't have AirPods in your ears, you are silent enough.

Silent enough to think. Silent enough to ponder. Silent enough to be aware. Silent enough to pay attention.

Silent enough to remind yourself of…wait for it…what you really do and don't give a crap about.

It's time to exercise.

Coming soon: You will get wrapped up in something that might be the opposite of what you care about.

If/when it happens, don't sweat it (I know, easier said than done). It's a great learning opportunity. Use the following exercise to help minimize those times in the future.

Here goes:

Write down what you care about. First figure it out, then ink it.

Next, remind yourself of what you wrote during your newfound moments of silence.

Will all of this completely shield you from getting bent out of shape by the jackass in the office?

Of course not, because the following scenario still can happen. Like, as soon as tomorrow.

You arrive to work under-slept, slightly hungover, stressed about something that has nothing to do with work, and that jackass coworker will get under your skin.

He'll get the best of you that day.

But this scenario could also happen. Like, as soon as tomorrow:

You arrive to work well rested, un-hungover [sic], relaxed and clear about what you give a crap about. On *that* day, you will laugh at the very same jackass coworker. No chance he's is getting under your skin (plus, let's face it, your skin is just the right thickness to prevent that from happening most of the time).

You will win that day.

Coming soon, with hard work, will be a life where you win most days.

Let's wrap this Truth.

So, did you do the exercise?

Do it…right now. Actually right now, in the margins of this book if necessary. Make a list of the things you care most about. Family? Friends? Work? Projects? Art?

Right now. Actually right now. Grab a pen and write, for crying out loud.

Good work.

Now, with that info locked down, and your priorities crystal clear, let's jump into the final Truth.

TRUTH SIX

Happiness is in the A to Y.

✴

In the intro, I promised a classic Domino's Pizza anecdote.

I keep my promises. And there's a point to this anecdote. Read on.

I've only been fired from one job in my life (so far). Domino's Pizza.

In high school I delivered pizzas in a little Texas suburb. Fun job, decent dough (pun intended), worked with my friends.

I continued working the summer after graduation until *just about* the time I left for college.

Just about.

I got the ax a few weeks before taking off for school, and here's why…

One night, my buddies and I were hanging out at the store, waiting for our next deliveries, when my girlfriend stopped by to say hi. As I got up and walked over to her, the manager (his very relevant name is coming) nonchalantly said, "If you go over to talk to her, I'm gonna fire you."

I thought he was kidding, and so over I went.

He wasn't kidding.

In a grandiose display of yelling and "insecure guy trying to be a tough guy in front of *my* friends" anger (remember Truth Two?), he canned me on the spot. I turned in the blue shirt and hat and headed home to break the news to my parents. As an aside, and to their credit, they didn't care.

A few weeks later I left Texas to start at UCLA.

That Christmas break I returned to Texas and headed over to Domino's to say hi to some of my friends who still worked there.

There I am, I'm hanging out in the strip mall parking lot, and who should come out but the very same manager. As soon as he saw me, he asked, "Hey, when are you gonna come back to work for us?"

Yeah, no.

Thanks for allowing me to share that very fond memory, and here's the point of the whole dang story.

The manager's name…

Journey.

I know, that was a long walk to the finish. But his name really, truly, was Journey.

And this was precisely when I started to hate the word "journey."

In other words, when someone says, "It's all about the journey, man!" I throw up a little in my mouth.

And yet…for this book…nay…for you…I'm pushing through my own "journey" reticence to write this Truth.

A Truth about…the journey.

So, I will now write about the journey.

Here I go. The journey. The journey.

The journey! I loves me a journey.

I'm fine now.

Don't worry about me; I'll get through this since it's something I really do care about.

(I know this because I read Truth Five after I wrote it.)

Turns out happiness *does,* in fact, exist in the journey.

If I could just...

Often we utter statements like the following:

> "If I could just win the lottery."
> "If I could just win the award."
> "If I could just get the big publishing contract."
> "If I could just get my dream job."
> "If I could just lose twenty pounds."
> "If I could just…if I could just…if I could just…"

To be clear, winning the lottery would likely bring some positives, just as awards, big contracts, and the wedding day can all kick ass.

But the good feelings associated with these events, when/if they occur, are fleeting. Momentary. Impermanent. They're all endgames. Goals or dreams achieved, for sure, but long-term happiness is found elsewhere.

Happiness in Z world.

Happiness—the permanent, sticking-around kind—is in the A to Y.

Not the Z.

Z is the lottery, Z is the raise, Z is the award.

Z's are exciting to get.

Getting to Z is awesome, but there's this other *little* thing we might want to attend to: the rest of our lives that we still have yet to live.

John Lennon nailed it with this quote: "Life is what happens while you're busy making other plans." What a beautiful and darling thing to say.

If you play your cards right.

If you play your cards right, by the time you get to Z, you can look back at A to Y and think, "Z? You're cool, but A to Y was frickin' awesome."

And then true happiness seekers will say, "I can't wait to get back to A."

Because resting on your laurels is for chumps.

Achievements are mere steps along the way.

Nothing happy about a fifty-year-old still talking about his high-school football days.

Achieve. Rinse. Repeat.

Achieve things. Reach your goals, get the stuff you want, and then…

Live more, do more, work more, love more.

Be more aware, be more engaged, be more yourself.

Act in spite of fear, work hard in spite of fatigue, be wrong in spite of an intense desire to always be right.

Try creating an A to Y that is as wonderful as possible.

Come back now, ya hear?

You will come back to this Truth often.

The other five Truths are wrapped up in this one because this Truth is your actual life. All the stuff that happens before the ultimate, final Z. You know, the Z that we're all afraid of and spend a lot of time and hard-earned money trying to avoid thinking about.

Z-elephant in Z-room. Z-Grim Reaper. Pardon my French.

I'm with you. It's not pleasant to think about.

Here's the best way to *not* think about something. Fill your head with something you'd rather think about.

Happiness hates vacuuming.

Here's the thing about happiness: It hates a vacuum.

You'll never be happy trying to *not* think or *not* do. If you try *not* to think about something, or try *not* to do something, a vacuum is created. And you'll have no idea what to fill it with.

On the other hand, the way to happiness, the way to reach the final Z with minimal regrets, is *to* think and *to* do.

Side note.

I don't care how old you are, how active you are, how financially successful or unsuccessful you are. You can *always* set goals and work toward them.

I direct a 50K trail ultra-marathon and have had sixty-plus- and seventy-plus-year-olds cross the finish line every year. Serious achievement, but I'm guessing they've been doing some good living to pull something like that off.

That's some serious A to Y business.

A fashion tip.

I'm all for defining your ideals and even setting big goals. Just one caveat: fashioning a gargantuan goal without fully understanding that it's not really about the goal itself will potentially lead you to feeling unfulfilled.

Best to illustrate with an example…

If you're eighty-five years old, setting a goal of running a sub-three-hour marathon and achieving it is, well, unlikely. And without understanding where happiness actually lives (in the journey, remember?), you'll be upset that you just can't hit the sub-three-hour pace.

On the other hand, realizing it's not really about the sub-three-hour marathon and more about being active means you can refashion the goal so that it's a better fit.

Something like walking six miles might just be the ticket.

Fine line between *big* goal setting and *too big* goal setting.

Ultimately it's whatever gets you moving toward the goal because it's the moving that counts.

Planned outcome obsolescence.

Know why your toaster will likely break in the next year or two? Planned obsolescence.

Planned obsolescence: An intentional plan to make something that will break in a short amount of time so that people will be forced to buy another.

Crappy, no?

But in the goal–setting arena, we can actually use planned obsolescence to our advantage…

Here's how:

Plan your life such that outcomes (awards, raises, goals reached) are mostly obsolete. In other words, set goals with the idea that they're a relatively insignificant part of your happy life.

In this way, the goal is simply there to provide you with something toward which to work.

And if you do, if you work and keep working, if, as soon as you reach a goal, you set out for another one, each outcome you reach will begin to matter less and less.

I'm not claiming it won't matter at all to hit your goals. It will matter, and it'll feel really good.

It just won't matter a ton.

The passion of happiness and that's a wrap.

When do you stop the cycle of hitting goals and immediately embarking on new goals?

Never.

Why?

Because of passion.

Passion is why.

A life of passion is a life well-lived.

Passion in the pursuit, the struggle, the action.

Passion is never the day you achieve a certain goal. Passion is in the getting to that day.

As much as you can, keep your head in the A to Y, and keep passion in your life. Always be moving toward something.

Always.

And then either continually hit your goals or die trying.

OUTRODUCTION

This is the big finish.

This outro is about how to use the truths. All six of 'em.

I wrote in Truth One that the other Truths, when sub-sumed into your being, become part of Truth One.

And I meant that.

Then, in Truth Six, I wrote that the other truths are all wrapped up in Truth Six.

And I meant that too.

The Great Overlap.

There is overlap in these Six Truths, and that's as it should be.

We are not partitioned beings. We're complex, intricate, intelligent, and nuanced.

But there's also a simplicity to us. Most of the stuff we really want in our lives is simple. The things that make us happy are quite simple, like family and friends that I wrote about in these pages.

Simple stuff.

Problem is we overcomplicate what needn't be overcomplicated and lose every time we do. Nutrition, exercise, socializing? Not complicated until we complicate them, thinking we have to micromanage food (measure, count, weigh) in order to eat healthier, micromanage movement (stats, heart rate monitors) in order to be physically fit, and spend a significant portion of our free time on social media to feel connected.

On the other hand, whenever we simplify our lives and remove the bullshit, we win.

The simplicity of happiness.

Don't let the simplicity of being happy be a deterrent.

One more time: Don't let the simplicity of being happy be a deterrent.

If achieving happiness sounds simple, that's because it is.

Don't confuse the simplicity of it with the hard work of it.

It *is* simple, but, for all the reasons in this book, it is not easy an easy thing to pull off. The challenges we're up against in today's world are vast.

It is our job to find a way to wade through our lives with both eyes open and on the ball as much as possible.

The why of happiness.

The real purpose of Six Truths is to make us *and* the world a happier place.

The more happy people, the better.

We can all achieve happiness by questioning, thinking, and strengthening each day. What you want to achieve plus the work of getting there are both part of the happiness equation. And as I wrote in Truth Four, you can't be happy if you're not constantly and consistently working for it.

All this is to say that all six Truths, once achieved and maintained, eventually become part of Truth One because the better *you* get, the better the example you set. And living this example changes the world for the better.

Simply stated: Work your ass off to express all Six Truths more and more each day.

And I'll write this one last time: It is good for *everyone* when you do.

You owe it to the world to be happy, and you for damn sure owe it to yourself.

And finally, for real...

Commit to living a life of thought, growth, passion, learning, adventure, and evolution and you will always feel alive, until, well, you're not.

And so...what I wish for you, for me, for everyone is that we strive to reach the very best in ourselves, and when we do, come to appreciate and understand that living a truly happy life is a very achievable and very worthy struggle.

For you, for me, for everyone.

BIBLIOGRAPHY & RESOURCES

Bibliography & References.

https://www.theatlantic.com/technology/archive/2013/06/skinner-marketing-were-the-rats-and-facebook-likes-are-the-reward/276613/

https://jamanetwork.com/journals/jamanetworkopen/fullarticle/2733430

https://www.nytimes.com/2019/06/03/well/family/teenagers-social-media.html

https://cummingsinstitute.com/news/surprising-impact-inflammation-mental-health/

https://www.psychologytoday.com/us/blog/expressive-trauma-integration/201905/inflammation-and-mental-health-symptoms

https://www.sciencedaily.com/releases/2017/06/170614134307.htm

https://www.npr.org/sections/health-shots/2015/10/25/451169292/could-depression-be-caused-by-an-infection

Kethledge, Raymond M. and Erwin, Michael S. *Lead Yourself First: inspiring leadership through solitude* (Bloomsbury Publishing, 2018)

Resources.

Except where otherwise noted, I am not connected financially to any of the resources below—as in, no kickbacks, affiliate deals, or commissions.

Other people's stuff (not financially connected to)

Wim Hof Method: the ten-week program I completed in 2017, and have been doing breathing and cold therapy every day since.

Found My Fitness Podcast (Rhonda Patrick): great interviews with scientists doing the actual research on cold and heat therapy and much more.

Oxygen Advantage by Patrick McKeown: good book, and I completed his instructor certification course in 2020.

Breath by James Nestor. Another good book on breathing techniques, including Wim Hof and much more.

My stuff (financially connected to)

My books:

Approaching the Natural: A Health Manifesto

Raising Healthy Parents: Small Steps, Less Stress, and a Thriving Family

My podcast:

What Sid Thinks on iTunes, Spotify, etc.

My coaching programs:

Small Steppers (my twelve-week online Awareness Based Habit Change program): **www.smallsteppers.com**

Small Step Intensive (my twelve-week private coaching program): **www.smallstepintensive.com**

My websites:

www.sidgarzahillman.com
www.thesidhillmanquartet.com

And finally:

Mendocino Coast 50K (the trail ultramarathon I founded and direct): **www.mendocinoultra.com**

About the author.

Sid Garza-Hillman holds a BA in Philosophy from UCLA, is a public speaker, podcaster, certified nutritionist and running coach, Oxygen Advantage® breathing instructor, and founder of Small Steppers. He is the Stanford Inn & Resort's Wellness Programs Director and Race Director of the Mendocino Coast 50K trail ultramarathon.

He lives on the Mendocino coast of California with his wife, three children, dog, cats, and horse.